A guide
to prayer
for busy people

Beryl and Michael Newman

Credits: design—Glenn Heinlein
cover and page 1—Kenneth Guentert.

ISBN 0-89570-196-0

First Printing, May 1980

Claretian Publications

A guide to prayer for busy people

Beryl and Michael Newman

This business of busyness

Today, more than ever, we need to take time out for prayer. The busier a person is—and who is not busy today?—the more important it is to make time for prayer and reflection on the business of life, to ponder the experiences it brings and try to understand them so as to be able to assimilate and integrate them. Otherwise there is danger of one's personality growing more and more fragmented and finally falling apart. Not that prayer is some kind of adhesive to put us together again when we are coming unglued. Far from it. Prayer, as it ought to be, not only keeps us in touch with ourselves but also with God.

It is when we contemplate God, particularly in his humanness, which is Christ, that we learn most about ourselves and the immense potential we have in union with him. Prayer is not something for God. It is for ourselves. It is not something we graciously or dutifully give to him, but a grace, a gift, he gives to us. Nor does our prayer add anything to him, although it adds immeasurably to us. Our lack of prayer does not diminish him, but a real turning away from prayer will in time lead to the disintegration of our mind and spirit.

More and more in this stressful age people tend to become workaholics and to search for both identity and self-esteem in their work. it may be well-nigh impossible to convince some Americans that "wasting time" in reflective rest may in some circumstances be highly productive, but even the most addicted busybodies can be encouraged to trim the fat from their schedules and learn to reduce mental cholesterol levels. In a way, the busier we are the more fortunate we are, for thus mental fatigue will sooner demand that we take time to be quiet and alone, to forget briefly what we are and are doing, and to remember who we are and why we live.

Those who are too busy to pray—and the group embraces all walks of life and lifestyles—are probably losing some perspective on the business of living as well as the business of praying. Most likely they are not seeing prayer as vital to human development and as integral to the whole process of life, but as a desirable practice that may or may not solve problems or lead to holiness. Prayer does not necessarily solve problems, although it may make us more aware of their causes and so enable us to deal with them more effectively. Nor does prayer make us holy. Only God is holy. What prayer does is make us human with the humanness of Christ, a humanness in touch with and touched by the divine.

We human beings are not a complete creation. None of us is born mature, at the peak of spiritual, physical, or psychological potential. We are always in process towards the fullness of being. This process should draw us closer and closer to union with God. There is in all of us a longing for God. When we turn to him in Christian prayer, we come in touch with all that we are and all that we might become, with all that we have come from and all that we are going towards. By integrating prayer, with its intimate consciousness of God, into daily living we cooperate with God's will and allow ourselves to become more closely formed to the image of God that lies waiting to be claimed in everyone.

In creating men and women with free will, God commissioned us, in effect, to complete his work of creation in ourselves, in cooperation with him and with an eye to his vision of what we are meant to be. Whatever else we do in a lifetime, the main purpose of our existence is to bring to reality this image God has of each of us, and in this way to realize his Kingdom in that part of life we call ours. We can do this only through prayer.

Prayer is as essential to human growth and health as, say, eating and breathing. Spiritual asphyxia and starvation can be just as harmful as the physical. Although we normally do not need to be reminded of the need to eat, we often have to be urged to set aside time to pray. When schedules are so hectic that there really is no time for meals, chances are we'll take a second to grab a snack. It should be like that with prayer.

Breathing is so integral to life that, however frantic the pace, the brain keeps on transmitting its signals and the lungs go on working so that we breathe almost involuntarily. One of the exercises promoted by the many programs to aid relaxation and meditation is to sit quietly and become aware of the act of breathing, watching the rise and fall of the chest, listening to the sound of expiring breath, filling the lungs slowly, and generally trying to raise our understanding of what breathing entails. When our minds are preoccupied we may be aware of breathing only in the occasional sigh, an almost involuntary moment of hiatus, of rest. Prayer, too, can become as instinctive as breathing.

Some things, like eating or breathing, may be considered obligations inherent in the fact of existence. We have not the right to choose whether to eat or breathe. We may choose to starve to death but only if we are prepared to violate the basic right to life. The same can be said about prayer. We may choose not to pray, but only if we are prepared to deny spiritual life.

We live for a purpose, and if we are to fulfill that purpose we must pray. Karl Rahner says, "No man can give himself the freedom he needs to respond totally to God. For this he needs to be set free by God himself, and he is set free only in prayer." We need to be freed from the instinctive, reactive elements of personality in order to enter into reflection and meditation on life and our place in it. And there are ways that even the busiest of us can find that freedom.

Obviously we are not talking about prayer only as an escape from the difficulties of the human condition. For Christians prayer has dimensions much greater than that. There is a way we ought to pray and need to pray, but it is not the form of prayer that matters. It matters only that we pray in a heightened awareness of the immediate presence of God and of the creative love that binds us to respond to him.

Hasty prayer is no prayer. If we are looking for personal fulfillment we have to start with some idea of how prayer affects ordinary life, quite apart from favors granted and petitions heard. And that means taking time to think about it. We should know what we are looking for in prayer and what to expect. Better still, we might enter into prayer with no expectations at all, for no one second-guesses God who is always the initiator in prayer.

Prayer is like love. Our expectations in love can never be the same as someone else's, because our experience is not the same as theirs nor are our needs the same. It is better to love without expectation except that of our own self-giving. No one can teach another to love or to pray. These are things we learn in the experiencing. But both love and prayer entail a distinct act of will and a more or less conscious decision.

Before we can love or pray as we ought, we need to bring that decision to the forefront of our consciousness and make it the impelling force of the way we live, so that it becomes integral to each day, each hour, every action. Prayer is not a choice for us but an imperative. "Pray constantly, and in all things give thanks, *because this is what God expects you to do.*" (1 Thess. 5:19)

To pray as Christians is to pray as Christ prayed, and the way we understand his prayer inevitably influences the nature of our own. As embodied in Jesus, prayer is itself love. When it is activated in personal relationships, it awakens a love which is itself prayer. There is a centric movement to Christian prayer. We enter God's presence in prayer, which activates his love in us so that we may liberate his love in all our relationships and return to him a love that is prayer.

Prayerful love or loving prayer is the one thing certain to be eternalized, for it comes from God and returns to him in an eternal circle of life. It is when prayer is not integrated into actual living that our loving is deficient. When Christians fail to love with the love that is prayer and to pray with the prayer that is love, they are in contradiction of Christ. Whether we are frantically busy or not, we must love and we must pray, for there is no other way to attain the humanness for which we were born.

Finding time to pray

There is a discrepancy between the way many of us talk about prayer and the way we practice it in our lives. On the one hand we may define prayer as a love-relationship with God, but on the other hand we complain of having little or no time to pray. Compare that with our human relationships and we can see the contradiction. Lovers, however busy they may be, are ingenious at finding time to be together. Foremost in their minds is the thought of each other. They will even forego food and drink to steal moments together. If they cannot be physically present they will spend hours on the telephone, often deep into the night, not speaking for long periods. It is enough to know that the other is at the other end of the line. On days when it is impossible to make some kind of contact the meaning goes out of life for them.

The difference between that and prayer is that God, unlike human lovers, does not importune us. He does not intrude himself upon our consciousness visually or aurally. He makes no demands, gives no reproaches. He waits in silence for our coming. When we are so busy about important things, like Martha at Bethany, it is easy to lose the time we meant to reserve for him, especially if we tie our prayer time to one specific point on the clock.

It is too easy to take God's silent and generous fidelity for granted when there are so many other things on our minds; and so, despite our best intentions, prayer may continue to elude us. The problem with finding time to pray is much the same as that of forming any other habit. We cannot superimpose a new routine over an old one, nor can we change an established habit of prayer without changing the way we think about prayer itself. Often the mental image we have of prayer, when we complain about lack of time for it, is one of secluded, uninterrupted hours, half-hours, or even quarter-hours set aside from the clamor of the day. And it is true, such times are important. Unfortunately, we usually try to secure them either in the early morning, when the rush and hustle of rising and leaving for work or getting children off to school may shatter the strongest resolution, or in the late evening when bone-weary and mentally fatigued.

8

Not everyone is able to take hours or half-hours to be alone and apart for prayer. For many, particularly mothers of young children, to secure even 15 minutes of undisturbed peace presents a problem. And since none of us can turn immediately and effectively from the secular to the spiritual on demand, additional time has to be allowed to settle down and fend off distraction. For those whose schedules are not only full but erratic, it makes better sense to commit oneself to a certain amount of time a day rather than one specific time-slot. If we pledge, say, 15 minutes morning and evening, it can be sandwiched in where it will fit—even if that means setting the alarm 15 minutes earlier or staying up 15 minutes later at night, or, as a last resort, praying in the bath.

If it is possible to devote the same time each day exclusively to concentrated prayer, well and good. If not, perhaps we should be more flexible on the question of when and where to pray. We do need some time each day, and a determination to persist in claiming it, even if it is disrupted more often than not. We need time to consider the direction of our lives and the way we are living them, and time to meditate on the life and word of Jesus and its meaning for us.

Broadly speaking, there really should not be a set time to pray, any more than there should be special times for loving. Both prayer and loving should run as continuous threads through the texture of our lives. But we do need to take time to express our feelings and get feedback. When a crowded schedule leaves us irritable and fatigued, it may be necessary to deliberately set apart time to be alone with a husband or wife, children or friends, so that our relationships do not suffer. We owe it to ourselves as well as others to take time to ease down and enjoy being with the other. In the same way, we must give some special time to prayer. The question is, how much time? And if there are incursions into the time allotted for God, is prayer lost for that day? If no thought has been given to communicating with him during the rest of the day we may have to chalk up another prayerless day.

Even when we have our special time all wrapped up and available, it may be difficult to withdraw from the concerns of work or family or community, and then prayer can become perfunctory, and prey to all kinds of distraction. But if awareness of God has permeated the day, the thought of him

9

is more likely to beckon us at day's end and be with us in the morning. Then, too, the distractions which might normally distress us would be less bothersome and could even form the content of prayer, because the events of the day have occurred within the awareness of his presence. As long as we are mentally active we will experience distraction in prayer, but God will accept this if we do not try to exclude him from what causes them. Anything can serve as a medium of prayer if it is imbued with a consciousness of God.

Problems arise when we make a division between prayer and actual living and have difficulty seeing a relation between the two. But things of the world are not alien to prayer. In fact, the things of human existence are precisely the matter of prayer. So, if we are to pray and pray more effectively, we have to find a way to bridge the gap between set-aside times and lard the day with God. *Larding,* as any old-fashioned cook will know, is threading bacon through the fibers of beef or venison to improve the flavor. We can lard the day with God by threading the awareness of him through all we do, so that there will be no abrupt transition to prayer but only an intensification of already existing communication.

There are dozens of moments during even the most frenetic day when we can break briefly from what we are doing almost without noticing it. These are moments we can use to recall the presence of God. Usually at such times our minds are anticipating the next thing we plan to do, so that the instant may slip by without our recognizing it for what it is, a moment of rest. But once alert to the possibility of these hidden intervals, we may discover all kinds of usable time. There are the pauses between one kind of work activity and the next, for instance, the break between one interview and another; the moment before settling to some project and the slight relaxation as it is completed; waiting for a telephone call to be put through; preparing to leave for lunch or for home. We can use these times to let the thought of God's presence touch and season what we are doing, saying, and being.

It is not so much a matter of taking time as of grasping available time. And there is no need to pray at these times, that is, to search for words or even to try to visualize God in the way we usually do. These are moments for nothing but basking in the recollection of God and sunning in his love.

One can't get away with saying, "Ah, but, my whole work is a prayer." Offering work to God is great but it does not meet the requirement of active prayer. We must repeatedly recall his presence, be still and know that he is God, anticipate his silent embrace, bask in the certainty of his love. When we do this, it is astonishing how many intervals during the day, which might otherwise have been filled with irritation and impatience, can be filled, instead, with spiritual alertness. We can become gatherers of time, spiritual ecologists recycling wasted moments. Think of the hours of enforced idleness we spend every day waiting for appointments; waiting in check-out lines; waiting for children to come out of school; waiting for the arrival of guests; waiting for rush-hour traffic to move; waiting for the minutes, half-hours, hours of commuting to pass! All these intervals that most of us spend amid disconnected sensations and day-dreamings are available and can be grasped to recall the presence of God and thus become times of prayer.

Of course, it is not easy to free our minds from preoccupations and immediately fall into meditation. Despite our good intentions, to turn our minds toward prayer is often like standing at an open door with guests who are reluctant to leave. We may become discouraged at our efforts to pray and think, "This is not for me." But it is! It is for each of us, whatever our circumstances. We can overcome such hurdles by turning our attention to our *incoming* guest, welcoming him by name. We can do this by briefly closing our eyes—well, maybe not in traffic jams—and slowly, mentally repeating the name of God. This is, after all, the way we normally call people to mind. It may seem strange at first, and perhaps pious, but as we grow used to the practice it is amazing how tensions and anxieties can abate when we thoughtfully repeat, "My God, my loving God."

Names are evocative and summon the awareness of the person they represent. Shakespeare, who knew human nature, has Juliet calling the name of Romeo in the night. Jesus, exhausted and alone on the cross, cried out in his need, "My God, my God." People newly bereaved often cry out the name of the dead person as if to deny that he or she is really gone. The ancient Jews considered the name synonymous with the person, and for them, to say someone's name was tantamount to being in the person's presence. That is why they did not enunciate the name of God; they believed that no one could enter his presence and live. Though Westerners do not as a rule share this concept, the prayerful repetition of the name of God does help us to concentrate on him and fill the moment with his presence.

We can call upon God at any time of day or night, whether resting or working. For not everything we do requires total concentration. Most of the time as we perform routine tasks, our minds are on something else. A mother preparing breakfast or school lunches may be thinking of a conversation she had with a neighbor the day before. Her husband, shaving in the bathroom, may be planning the morning's work or balancing the family budget. Their hands are transmitting one set of data to the brain, but their minds are sending something else. Our memory banks, being the efficient computers they are, store away both sets of information. Chances are that the next time the husband and wife repeat the routine task, the thought of the neighbor will flit through her mind and the budget or work plan through his. If that time had been grasped for prayer, every repetition could serve as a built-in memory nudge.

Washing dishes, changing the baby's diaper, taking a coffee break, running a bath or shower—each day there are many such mundane, repetitive, automatic acts that barely involve our consciousness. They can be vehicles of prayer, for they all afford us at least a few seconds pause, time enough to let our thoughts rest in God and remember why we live.

We may complain, with some irritation, that we really do not need to be constantly reminded to recollect the presence of God. We claim the thought of him is always "at the back of my mind." And that, alas, is just the point! The thought of God does lurk on the periphery of our awareness a great deal of the time, often barely penetrating our consciousness. We give him the same kind of inattentiveness we give to routine or reflex actions, the kind we do not remember later on. Like the young mother who, deep in conversation with a friend, responds to her child's whining by lifting him on to her lap without a break in concentration. Later, as he clambers down, she will look at him and smile. Afterwards she might recall only the moment of the smile. His cry and her automatic response will simply not have registered. A young teacher of handicapped children, being interviewed on the local television station, charmed viewers by reaching out to a child who had come to stand beside her and lovingly brushing his hair from his forehead. Her eyes did not leave the interviewer's face, but as the interview ended, she turned and smiled at the boy. Later she did not recall her affectionate gesture, but she did remember the boy's face as she smiled at him and his answering smile.

It is quite possible to carry the thought of God in that kind of marginal focus, but we, too, need to turn and smile at him to become fully conscious of his presence. The smile of the heart, or as the Eastern mystics call it, the prayer of the heart, need be no more than the whispered, "My God, my God." It takes just a moment to close our bodily eyes and open the inner eye to contemplate our source and slowly, deep within ourselves, say his name. If there is more time, and our attention begins to wander, we can repeat the name again and again and notice how tension starts to ease and calmness takes over. Our breathing may slow and deepen too, adding to the sense of relaxation and peacefulness.

A retreat director once told a number of priests that if they would faithfully give "three minutes a day to doing absolutely nothing but rest in the awareness of God" he would guarantee that in six months their spiritual life would be transformed. Three minutes is a long time for busy people to do nothing consciously, but there are many short pauses hidden in every day. How we use them is our choice.

Some people feel more comfortable saying the name of Jesus, particularly if they have some experience of the charismatic style of prayer. There is nothing new in this practice. A centuries-old tradition, especially in the East, is the Jesus prayer: "Jesus, Son of the living God, have mercy on me, a sinner." It is often referred to as an aid to contemplative prayer. Today more and more people are praying the name of Jesus and receiving great benefit from it. Jesus always leads to the Father, and when we pray the Father's name we pray the prayer of Christ himself.

What matters most is that these pauses are not filled with words. While we are talking, we are not listening or meeting ourselves in the silence. The shorter the prayer the better, the more repetitive the better, in this stolen, fleeting time. It is the way of lovers who repeat each other's name just to cherish the sound, just because they love, and because in holding the name they hold each other. There are times for talking things out, times for discursive prayer; but there are times, too, for the prayer of just being. Just-being prayer is not a time for solving problems, airing anxieties, and so on. It is time to step aside from all the hassle and hustle to rest in God and allow his peace to remind us of who we really are and what life is about. It is time "wasted," left empty to make room for the healing power of prayer to seep into our being and restore our center of calm. It is time gathered to ourselves for the sake of ourselves, those inner selves so sorely in need of breathing space and stillness.

Everyone has a need for space. According to social scientists, pure physical space for moving and living is immensely important for human development. The right kind and proper amount of space has an effect upon our peace of mind, attitudes, and actions. We have even greater need for spiritual space, in which we can take the long view of things and feel the breeze of the Spirit. We need such space to learn an openness which makes possible an honest evaluation of ourselves. We can then come to accept God's will for us.

Fortunately we can make spiritual space even when physical space is limited. People who somehow find themselves physically confined manage to do this all the time. Men and women have prayed profoundly and discovered great freedom by making spiritual space for themselves even in the confinement of prisons, hospitals, or other institutions. We can have as much spiritual space living in an apartment as in a mansion, traveling by Volkswagen as by Lincoln Continental, spending a day in the kitchen as on the beach. Doors and windows, physical or spiritual, remain closed only if we do not open them.

A saint, whose name I have forgotten, was quoted in a biography as saying that his spiritual life and relationship to God were more real to him than the people and environment of his daily life. This may have been so, but that is not the kind of spiritual space in which Jesus lived. His kind of spiritual space not only left room for every person he met and an acute awareness of his surroundings, it also imbued him with a sensitivity towards the human condition and the needs of individuals that has never been equalled. It is this kind of freedom and compassionate alertness that prayer is meant to awaken in those who are not selfish with spiritual space when they find it.

And once the hunt for time and space is on, the challenge can become exciting. We may grow miserly, snatching at vacant moments in a kind of spiritual gluttony and then, as prayer does its work in us, discover its strengthening touch firming the flab of our lives. All this takes time but, after all, we are in the conservation business.

Many activities we would not previouly have associated with prayer may suddenly present themselves as golden opportunities. One housewife was troubled by the amount of time and care she gave to her garden, and the little time she gave to prayer. She spoke to a priest about it. He replied in a parody of an old Jesuit joke: "It would not be right to garden while you are praying, but there is no reason why you should not pray while gardening." Her favorite prayer happened to be the rosary, and she resolved her problem by calculating how many Hail Marys it took for her to adequately water her roses, how many for the dahlias, which potted plants could do with an Our Father, and so on. "And do you know," she said later, "I feel the presence of God so strongly now among my flowers, it is as though he touched me."

A farmer salvages the 40 minutes or so it takes him every night to fill the water trough for his animals. "I have to stand there and wait for the tank to fill and being alone under the stars in the quiet of the night, God seems very close. I don't really pray in words or even actively meditate, but just rest in the moment and the thought of him. I get a great feeling of peace, and everything somehow falls into place. It's my most precious time of day." A young woman, a high-school teacher, has the short prayer form down to a fine art. At various times during the school day she simply cries out voicelessly, "God?" rather as a child playing in another room will call to a parent "just to know you are there."

Each person will find his or her own times and ways of making contact. One prayer may be very meaningful at one

15

time, and another prayer later, but a person's whole outlook on life can be affected by saying one little prayer frequently. An elderly woman credits the petition, "My Jesus, be not my judge but my Savior" with completely removing her fear of death and raising her confidence in her own salvation. A young person meets almost every challenge with "Lord, let me be what you need me to be and do what you want me to do" and then goes on to do what seems best. Another always-effective prayer is "Let your will be done (in this or that), and help me to accept it."

People who spend a lot of time commuting between home and work have ready-made occasions to pray. Depending on the length of the journey, a commuter can pray the prayer of the heart, the Jesus prayer, or the rosary; can meditate on Scripture; or play tapes of psalms, or hymns. As life-long choir singers we were raised on the adage that a prayer sung is a prayer doubly said. But to sing while commuting might call forth some comment from fellow travellers on a bus or train. Praying the Our Father in the "rythmical-recitation" way suggested by St. Ignatius or pausing to consider each phrase, would easily fit into a 10- or 15-minute run.

If we have really pressing matters to think about, our prayer may take the form of viewing them from the perspective of our relationship with God. Are these matters as important as they appear? Do they reflect a truly Christian viewpoint? How do they look when we stand with them in the presence of God? If our reactions, feelings, and ideas make us uncomfortable in his presence, perhaps they need to be examined more carefully.

Insomnia is probably one of the most frustrating things to handle. Morton Kelsey tells how much he was bothered by insomnia until a psychologist friend asked, smiling, "Has it ever occurred to you that someone might be trying to get through to you? Don't you remember how God called Samuel in the night?" From then on he discovered his sleepless hours to be prime time for prayer. No noises of children, no telephone, no interruptions of any kind.

The worries we fret about at night can assume mammoth proportions and push sleep farther and farther away. Prayed over, they are often diminished, and we are sufficiently freed from anxiety to find the solutions or acceptance that have been eluding us.

A simple pastime like walking in the country or on the beach is another example of prime time for prayer. How many of us express our pleasure in the beauty surrounding us? The wonders of nature *are* incredibly wonderful and as we marvel at them it is a small step to murmur, "My God, how great you are!" The companionship of a friend on occasion can also bring a person to prayer. "Oh Lord, I genuinely thank you for the presence of this friend. Thank you for the things we share and the love that lets us respect our differences."

Reading, listening to, or watching the news can be prayer time. Attending a concert or listening to the stereo, witnessing the performance of some extraordinary talent are all times open to prayer. Even the car wash has possibilities. There are a number of analogies to be drawn, such as cleanliness of spirit and the need for periodic scrubbing. Another fruitful source of prayer is people-watching, reflecting on the many forms of the image of God and the authenticity of his presence in them all—even those who, as Mother Teresa would say, represent Christ in a "most distressing guise."

If there is time to work, time to play, time to talk, time to love, time to enjoy the blessings of life or endure its pains, then there is time to pray, for all that constitutes life can be an occasion of prayer.

Beginners in prayer

One of the things about prayer that is both heartening and disheartening is that we are all beginners in the sight of God. Heartening, because no one need ever feel inadequate or ineffective when his or her own prayer seems to be less advanced than someone else's; disheartening because there is no level at which one can settle back in the assurance of finally having made it.

There is no end to prayer, but a series of beginnings and beginning again. God takes our beginnings, develops them, and brings them to perfection in himself. We tend to make a mystery of prayer, but when we come right down to it prayer is primarily a matter of consciously entering into God's presence and giving him our attention, talking to him if there is something to talk about, and sitting comfortably in silence if there is not. Most of the time, prayer is a sharing of the joys and problems of life, the ambitions and hopes we cherish, the pains and pleasures we experience. It is more like a kaffeeklatsch than a meeting with the chairman of the board, more like the endless communication of real friends than the mastery of interpersonal techniques.

When friends get together they seldom give much thought to what they are going to say to each other. Usually they just share whatever happens to be on their minds at that time. Often they talk out frustrations and difficulties. Sometimes they pass time chuckling over trivia. It does not matter so much what they say to each other as that they are together in a relationship that is accepting, nonthreatening, and mutually loving.

Prayer is like that. The content of our prayer is not as important as the way we approach God. Beginning to *say prayers* is no problem. All one needs is a book of prayers, a rosary, or a special need in our lives—and God knows we seldom run out of needs! Beginning to *pray* is something else, because it centers on relationship. We can talk for a great length of time to someone and yet not really communicate. In the same way, we may spend an hour or more saying prayers and not really pray at all. On the other hand, we may do exactly the same thing and pray deeply, because we are filling the time with longing for God and delight in his presence. By the same token, we might meditate for long periods, using Zen or Yoga methods, and still not really pray.

Prayer is a very individual thing and is not dependent on techniques or exercises. We pray primarily in our *desire* to pray and in our yearning for God. Nevertheless, in prayer as in any other form of communication, there are ways in which we can learn to grow more receptive and perceptive, usually through a relaxed alertness, or alert relaxation. We practice such techniques every day in our interaction with one another.

A visitor arrives at the home or office and the first thing we do is to try to make him or her feel comfortable and easy in our presence. "Sit down," "Make yourself comfortable," "Would you like a cup of coffee?" Then we usually spend a few minutes settling down—talking about the weather or the traffic or some other neutral topic. These pleasantries are meant to set the other person at ease and facilitate communication. They also give the other person time to change gears and become present to us, and for us to do the same for the visitor. Then we can get down to business.

Between friends there are other little rituals such as "Take your coat off," "Put your feet up," "There's a beer in the fridge." All of which is saying, "Make yourself at home and feel accepted." That accomplished, we are free to ask, "So, what's new?"

Many of the techniques of prayer perform the same function of inviting relaxation and a sense of openness and trust. For the most part they are little rituals that someone, perhaps a saint like Teresa of Avila or Ignatius Loyola, has found effective and which have then been adapted for wider use. These techniques are not meant to be mandatory exercises, merely efforts to help people who want to pray more effectively than they have been doing.

Some techniques, like reflecting on a passage of the Scriptures, are commonsense ways to learn more about the nature of God through the words and works of his Son or the salvation history of his people. Others, like deep rythmic breathing, are probably based on the realization that in times of calm meditative prayer, one's breathing is affected. We do not have to tie ourselves to one particular way of praying. On the contrary a set way of praying may in time lead to indifference and boredom. We can and should pray with all the variety of our being.

There is the prayer of friendship in which we feel free to comment to God on the personal, intimate things that are so important to us and to ask for help and support.

There is the prayer of lovers, with all the security of knowing that we are cherished and cared for and may expect unreasonably generous favors from the One who loves us.

There is the prayer of childhood with its acknowledgement of our total dependency and our limited awareness and knowledge.

There is the prayer of the colleague, the co-builder of the Kingdom, the instrument of the Word, the tool that must be kept honed and clean.

There is the prayer of the seer to whom God is present in visual things: the people around us, the trees and mountains and valleys, the oceans and rivers, animals and birds.

There is the prayer of the hearer, which speaks of God in music and song and the sounds of the world.

There is the prayer of the writer, who in poetry and prose writes of what lies too deep to be spoken.

There is universal prayer, with its awareness of the bond connecting all human beings and their responsibility for all creatures.

We are variable creatures, and prayer is unlikely to satisfy us long if we always pray in the same way. Most of us will pray differently at different times, depending on our mood, just as we vary our other activities. There are times, for instance, when we feel like talking seriously, others when it is more satisfying to spend a while in harmless gossip. There are times when we prefer to read quietly, others when we would rather listen to music. There are times for heart-searching and for pouring out what we find there, times for working through problems and wrestling with crises, times for silence and just being. Taking our feelings to prayer makes good sense. It is one of the most effective ways of coming to understand and integrate them. Prayer is not out of place in any setting, and there is nothing to be gained by denying one's feelings. After all, we know how we feel and so does God, so who is the play-acting aimed at?

Prayer begins with the *desire* to pray. obviously we have to want to pray and to want to enough to do something about it. We are all familiar with the half-wish, the good intention: "I must call Mary, when I have time." "We really should call on John, sometime." "I've been meaning to visit her, but. . ." Or, "I really want to pray but somehow. . ." So this first step moves us from the "I ought," and "I'll try," to "I will." There is nothing like repetition to root a desire in the subconscious where it can direct our actions, and there is room here for a spoken or unspoken expression of the will to pray.

Getting together is the next step. That is, setting a date, making an appointment, taking time, finding physical space if possible, spiritual space always.

Third, there is the settling-down period, the process of relaxing and letting tensions flow away. This is where deep breathing and a conscious relaxation of both mind and body can help. There are a number of ways to achieve this and practically any of the many techniques being promoted today can be used. Actually, the simple command to oneself "Now, relax," may be enough for some people.

Those who are really busy and therefore subject to steady pressures know the value of relaxation. We are more effective and accomplish more then we approach our work—or for that matter, our play, and certainly our prayer—in an alert relaxedness. It is not the amount we have to accomplish so much as the haste and anxiety with which we approach it that makes us tense. In a state of relaxation we do not place unnecessary obstacles in the way of our thinking and feeling. We may not be ready for a spiritual shedding of jacket and shoes, but everyone can learn to savor a moment of respite and begin to unwind.

There are any number of preliminaries or opening prayers that may serve as our introduction. Perhaps a simple recitation of the Hail Mary or the Our Father will bring just that touch of familiarity we need to feel comfortable and open to God. Others might use some greeting like "Dear Lord, here I am again. Be with me and bear with me." This might be the time to read a passage from Scripture or a favorite prayer or poem.

A quiet reflection on the sign of the cross and the way we become united with the Trinity when we pray in the name of the Father, Son, and Spirit can move us from the threshold to the heart of prayer. Or, if there is some urgent matter to thrash out, "Sweet Jesus, I need your help!" For some of us this may be the time for a quiet centering in on ourselves, without words or conscious thought. Or we may prefer to sing or think about some hymn or tune that has meaning for us. In mental song we do not have to make allowances for the quality of our voices.

Whatever enhances relaxation and a sense of intimacy will do. It is *our* comfort, *our* openness, *our* easiness, *our* expectancy that matters, and anything that promotes that is not only suitable but desirable.

From there it is a short step to the nitty-gritty of sharing prayer, which will vary with our moods and our needs. We may need simply to take something to Christ and look at it in his presence. We may desperately need help in some dilemma. We may feel the urge to share some joy or happiness and let God and ourselves know how deeply grateful we are. There may be promises to make, favors to ask.

Many people find it helpful to write out prayers. Sometimes this helps them clarify and crystallize thoughts and feelings they have not been able to bring to the forefront of their consciousness. Some may object that writing makes prayer too self-conscious, that what is written is meant to be read, and that can militate against honesty in prayer. But there is a case to be made for both writing and not writing, depending on what makes prayer more natural and fluent for the one concerned.

After all, most of the great devotional prayers are prayers written by people who have profound love of God and abandonment to his will. And writing one's thoughts or feelings can be effective against the ever-present irritation of distractions. No one, not even the holiest saint, seems to have been free of distractions in prayer, and at times distractions may point to a problem or a solution we have been ignoring.

If distractions bother us, it helps to take time to look at them and decide whether they are important or just aimless daydreaming. If they appear trivial it should not be too difficult to turn from them. If some valid concern about work or family underlies them, this is a good time to think about the situation and pray about it. An anxiety or fear may be demanding attention, and what better place and time to come to grips with it than in prayer?

Of course, there are times when our greatest distraction is a wild sense of exhilaration and happiness which makes it hard to concentrate on anything, even prayer of thanksgiving. But the experience of joy is itself a form of prayer, and to enjoy it fully in the awareness of God is to pray fully. Prayer is meant to be tied to the things of daily life, and every event, every human encounter, every success or failure, every aspect of living may be an occasion of and an expression of prayer.

Most of the time prayer will take the form of petition. That is true of most people most of the time and all people some of the time. Everyone is in need of help of one kind or another and the person who wants to pray is usually very much aware of this. Petitional prayer is an expression of our dependency on God's love and continuing grace. St. Thomas Aquinas considered it the highest form of prayer, in that it implies deep faith, strong love, and great hope.

Generally there is not much problem finding material for such prayer—there is so much we need and want. But there is a proper way to petition. Prayer is always entering into union with God, to a lesser or greater degree, and that means coming to perceive both our needs and our responsibilities in a wider perspective.

When we invite God into our lives and ask his help he will give us the grace to do what is necessary, but he will not do it for us. He respects our autonomy and never imposes anything on us, not even goodness. So in praying for our needs or someone else's, we undertake also the responsibility of doing all we can to meet them ourselves in the confidence of God's support.

It is interesting to notice how often the phrase "Lord, *make* me. . ." occurs in prayer. Make me holy, or kind, or charitable or successful. It is as though we expect God to imbue us with virtue despite ourselves. But to pray "Lord, *help* me" to become more loving, forgiving, or kind, and so on, acknowledges that while we desperately need help, the brunt of change rests on our willing cooperation with his will.

Some people make a practice of universalizing their

prayer, by reminding themselves of the corporate responsibility of Christians for all human beings. For instance, they would extend a personal prayer for healing such as "My loving God, let your healing power rest on my daughter and relieve her pain," by saying, "and touch all who suffer and are in need of healing today."

If we were to pray, "Lord, grant success to the work of our hands and to all who labor honestly and sincerely," it might put a couple of things in perspective for us. We can add the universal dimension to all our prayers:

- for the dead: "and all who will die or have died this day";
- for the bereaved: "and all who have suffered the loss of those they love today";
- for newlyweds: "and for all who are starting out on married life";
- for new babies: "and all new life today."

Of course, praying for the sick, dying, or the bereaved does not relieve us of the necessity of offering some evidence of our concern in a visit, telephone call, letter, card, or gift of flowers. And praying for strength for a friend in crisis also demands that we should be prepared to offer a strong arm or shoulder if needed. Likewise, praying about world catastrophes puts us in the position of having to do something about them, even if it is only writing to our senator or filling out a check. Petitional prayer is not an evasion but an affirmation of our responsibility to ourselves and others.

There is, too, the question of purification of our motives. We need to reflect on the long-term impact of the events we so urgently desire and consider the consequences the fulfilment of our requests might have on other people and situations. In many hidden and subtle ways we might harm or distress someone else in pursuing our own apparent good. Petitional prayer, undertaken thoughtfully and carefully, will inevitably lead to a broadening of our concept of what is both good and necessary.

One valid expression of prayer that is often overlooked is laughter. Laughing with God is not an image that comes immediately to mind when we visualize Christians at prayer. Usually a community at prayer looks more like a crowd of mourners at a funeral than joyful celebrants of the reality of Christ risen and living among us. It is only very recently that we have grown accustomed to the idea that laughter in church is not sacrilegeous. And yet we love to hear laughter and are easily infected by it. Since we are made in the image of God, surely we can presume laughter must be pleasing to him too.

There are those who find themselves frequently laughing aloud when contemplating God's action in their lives. "God has such a droll way of answering my prayers, it just makes me laugh all the time," a middle-aged woman confessed a little shyly during a retreat. "And sometimes just knowing he is around and loving me is so delightful I can't help laughing."

Laughter can be as effective a method of praise and thanksgiving as the most inspiring psalm and, as the Apostles demonstrated at Pentecost, not at all irreverent. We do God a disservice, surely, if we imagine that only solemnity and long faces are acceptable to him, when it is he who has given us the gifts of joy and laughter.

Thanks and praise traditionally and rightly conclude most prayer times. We may thank God either formally, by saying "O Lord, we thank you and we praise you," or informally, by saying "You are so good to me, how can I thank you enough?" Or, as one rather unconventional devotee put it, "God, you really are something else!" Or we may offer the silent gratitude of our hearts.

Beginning to pray is like beginning to love. At first there may be setbacks; we may have to feel our way; we may feel inadequate or ineffective, but the inadequacy is in our eyes, not God's. Prayer is always a healing process and a growth. Through it we come to the fullness of humanity and learn who we are, where we are going, and why. As in all relationships we must learn to risk vulnerability, honesty, and, therefore, pain. But where there is real progress in prayer it is paralleled by an increased ability to initiate and sustain loving relationships and to accept ourselves and others more completely.

God comes to us when and how we are best able to receive and assimilate him. He is always the initiator of prayer, so we should neither expect too much nor be satisfied with too little in prayer. As a retreat master told a group of candidates for the diaconate, "Pray as well and as often as you can and then you can expect everything from God!"

Sometimes something will happen to accelerate the process of prayer. Our timetable is not God's and perhaps we may be lagging a bit, or may be a little denser, more obdurate than he will countenance, and then an experience of depth may knock us off kilter and precipitate us to where God really wants us. Generally that is on our knees, humble and stripped of our comfortable illusions. But most of the time there will be a gradual unfolding, a growing intimacy and a slow revelation of ourselves to ourselves and of what God wants of us. This comes inevitably when we take time to rest in his presence and let his love do its work in us.

Creative use of prayer time

Presuming we have managed to corner a wedge of time, a precious several minutes to devote exclusively to prayer, what is the best way to use it? There are probably almost as many opinions on that as there are people who pray. But everyone agrees on one thing, the first step is to relax. If the place where we are praying is more or less public, this may simply mean sitting still and allowing the muscles to unclench. We spend far too much time clenched up. Even our toes and eyelids clench in reaction to anxiety and tension.

The first move toward relaxation, for most people, is to uncross legs or ankles and open fists; to let arms and legs hang loosely and to begin to breathe slowly and deeply, so that the chest moves in easy rhythm. Then concentrate on relaxing the face and neck. Fortunately, relaxing exercises are so "in" these days that no one is going to call for a strait-jacket if someone is moving his or her head up and down, left and right, and in circles to loosen neck muscles. We are not always aware of the extent to which we clench our faces. Taut jaw and cheek muscles, and screwed up eyelids are an automatic response to stress. In turn, these tensions induce greater mental tension and so we become locked in a vicious cycle. Chances are that by the time we have succeeded in relaxing our eyelids, our toes are standing to attention again and our calves and thighs doing isometrics. So, start all over again—what else is there to do with that reserved time?

Even if the place where we pray is secluded and we are alone, it may take just as much effort to relax. Some people are helped by lying prone or by curling up on a bed or the floor; others by walking; yet others by sitting, and so on. There is, however, something to be said for kneeling when it comes to prayer. Kneeling was a natural position of prayer long before it became enshrined in the rubrics of liturgy. Left to itself, the body will usually express in its own way what is going on in a person's mind and emotions, and falling to one's knees has, since remembered time, been the first in-stinctive movement towards prayer. It is an attitude that has many things to say to and about an open mind.

When the opportunity to pray presents itself, the place where we are is the place to pray; but all the same, there are places which seem more conducive to prayer. By all means, pray more frequently there. Many of us prefer to pray before the Blessed Sacrament or at least in a chapel or church. Others experience greater freedom and feel a closer relationship to God in open spaces close to nature. Some immediately seek the privacy of a bedroom or study. It is a matter of trial and choice. If we pray often in one particular place, that becomes a place of and for prayer. Places that are regularly prayed in retain and exert a special power of their own. There is a kind of residual effect, a spiritual force that influences and evokes prayer. If we pray in a new place, in time it, too, will become a place of prayer.

Once we are unclenched, stilled, and breathing calmly, we are ready to pray creatively, that is, to pray in such a way as to bring into being in us the qualities and orientation of mind that will lead to greater humanness and closer union with God. There are many, many ways to do this. We may choose traditional prayers, those we know by heart and have recited most of our lives, or spontaneous ones, which generally means those we make up on the spot. But the lines of division are by no means clear-cut. Everyone who prays does so both traditionally and spontaneously. Not everyone, however, does justice to the wealth of ways of praying available. Traditional prayer, for instance, implies much more than saying the rosary or the Stations of the Cross—though both of these may be creative. Traditional prayer calls upon centuries of experience of God and humankind to help expand our limited vision.

Praying spontaneously does not always mean what one might imagine. It may be most effective when we use the words of the psalms or some rote prayer. Sometimes, many times, others have said better what our hearts long to say, and then we may pray just as spontaneously when we use their words. Jesus' prayer on the cross was no less spontaneous because the words he cried out were from the Twenty-second Psalm.

Spontaneous prayer should evolve from a reflection upon personal experience of life with both our own and God's action in it. We pray spontaneously any time we enter into thoughtful conversation with God, whether privately or in community. It should never be understood to mean a hastily composed peroration to fill a silence in a prayer gathering, nor a self-conscious utterance to impress others and ourselves with our piety and facility with words. Nor is *spontaneous* synonymous with *aloud*. Vanity often ensures that the prayers we ad-lib in a group are anything but spontaneous or even real prayers. They may be more structured and formal than any we learned by heart as children. The whole idea of spontaneous prayer seems to exert a certain pressure on some prayer groups. Even when the suggestion for spontaneous prayer is couched in permissive terms, or is, perhaps, unspoken, the invitation acts like a command, and people may plunge into speech more in the spirit of cooperation than in the spirit of prayer.

Sometimes a personal reaction to real or imagined expectations can lead someone to address God in quite ludicrous terms. In a group session when spontaneous prayer was invited, a man who happened to be leader of a local parish prayer group started with, "O great and wonderful Lord, fount of wisdom, help of the poor and guide of the wayward, rod of Jesse, staff of David, King of all, we praise thee and we thank thee and humbly ask. . .etc., etc." No doubt he was quite sincere, but one wonders what his reaction would be if his own child had approached him with "O great and powerful Father, owner of the Ford and Chevrolet, keeper of the keys and provider of gasoline, help, and sustenance of your children, I praise thee and thank thee and humbly ask that thou wouldst vouchsafe to make available to thy lowly servant one of the cars for the movies tonight."

Prayer should reflect our relationship with God, and as Christians we approach him as a loving Father, not as a tribal chief who demands litanies of praise to accompany the utterance of his name. Of course, one ought to pray in both praise and thanksgiving and in awareness of the greatness of God, but not in terms that put distance between us because of their foreignness to our normal speech. Any time we take a long loving look at God and speak to him in our hearts, we are praying spontaneously, whether our speech is silent or vocal. Many people who shy away from spontaneous prayer nevertheless practice it daily in privacy. It is just another example of the confusion that can result from categorizing and over-defining prayer.

Usually there is no dearth of things to pray about. People are always in need, if not of one thing, then of another; if not a need of our own, then someone else's. But the best time for prayer is when we feel we have nothing to pray for. Then we are free simply to enjoy resting with God, dreaming awhile about his love and generosity and relishing it. This is hard for busy people to do. We are so used to filling every crack of time that we feel guilty when not doing something, even when at prayer. So, if we are not to "babble like the pagans," we will probably be grateful for a little guidance. Everyone needs help with prayer at one time or another, and at such times we have to be willing to reach beyond ourselves to others whose experience of God and reflection on it has been profounder than our own, and let them lead us. The Scriptures, especially the psalms, the prayers of saints, meditations and writings by contemporary thinkers, songs, and poems can all be used to prompt and stimulate our own prayer.

Take, for instance, the prayer from Cardinal John Henry Newman's *Meditations and Devotions:*

> Dear Jesus, help me to spread your fragrance everywhere I go; flood my soul with your spirit and life; penetrate and possess my whole being so utterly that all my life may only be a radiance of yours; shine through me and be so in me that every soul I come in contact with may feel your presence in my soul; let them look up and see no longer me but only Jesus! As I come from you—as I am made through you—so, my God, may I at last return to you and be with you for ever.

It is so completely Christian a prayer that one could hardly improve upon it, so why try? It says all there is to say in truly creative prayer. During an exercise when a number of men were asked to meditate on this prayer one said, "Well, it's very beautiful, but I am just not there yet. I can't aspire to this kind of self-forgetfulness." The leader looked at him. "Well," he said, "that's why it is a prayer." But if

Newman's vision seems too remote for us to be comfortable with, there are others, like that of St. Francis of Assisi:

> Lord, make me an instrument of your peace; where there is hatred let me sow love; where there is injury, pardon; where there is doubt, faith; where there is despair, hope; where there is darkness, light; and where there is sadness, joy.

Or the one attributed to St. Ignatius of Loyola:

> Dearest Lord, teach me to be generous; teach me to serve you as you deserve; to give and not to count the cost; to fight and not to heed the wounds; to toil and not to seek for rest; to labor and not to ask for any reward, save that of knowing that I do your will.

It is not necessary always to pray in our own words, only to pray in our own hearts.

There will be times in the course of a lifetime when we simply have no words; times when we enter into an area of the spirit where we have not been before; times of suffering or enlightenment which are too new for us to verbalize, and then the only release may come through someone else's prayer tumbling up from memory. A mother, stunned and in terrible anguish of spirit following the suicide of her son, found strength to endure only in the repetition of Psalm 130:

> Out of the depths I cry to you, O Lord! Lord hear my voice!. . . If you, O Lord, mark iniquities, who can stand? But with you is forgiveness. . .

A young nun, very much into spontaneous, unstructured prayer, admitted that in moments of severe personal need she found herself constantly drawn to the Hail Mary. Another person, dedicated to extemporaneous prayer, at a time of intense suffering found solace in repeating the second half of the Hail Mary: "Holy Mary, Mother of God, pray for us sinners." In this postconciliar era there are some to whom praying the Hail Mary seems like rankest conservatism, but pain, particularly agony of spirit, has a way of unlocking mental doors one thought were rusted closed. This points again to the need for openness in our approach. We can never be sure where prayer will lead us, so we might as well be prepared to accept whatever comes, even when our own experience seems to contradict another's.

One person may move from being tongue-tied to triumphant utterance; the next from verbosity to silence. A friend related once how her own progression in prayer was parallelled by her physical approach towards the altar. "It was a time when my whole world had been overturned and I was in great personal need. At first I knelt at the back of the church, praying very volubly with many pleas and supplications. But as days went by, I kept feeling I had to get closer to God and began praying through Christ and then directly to the Father. At the same time, without really thinking about it, I moved from pew to pew, making my way up the church. Finally I found myself before the Blessed Sacrament and quite bereft of words, just kneeling there in a great yearning towards God. I am a very vocal person and it took me some time to realize that, for the first time in my life, when I had nothing to say I was really praying."

On the other hand there are people who feel painfully inadequate at verbalizing prayers and need some kind of help to express feelings only partly understood. This is where reading or reciting prayers can be such a boon. No one need feel ashamed or out-of-it using this kind of aid. Even St. Theresa of Avila, a formidable practitioner of prayer, recommended it. It does not matter which prayers one uses. Prayers do not date. There are variations in literary style, of course, but that may only mean reading *you* for *thee,* and *your* for *thine.* Certainly the things we pray about today are no different from what people have prayed about for generations. The sum of human experience is not so varied that someone has not been before where we are now, however unique our condition may appear to us.

The psalms, for instance, have been prayed for centuries and when we pray them it is in communion with all those countless thousands who have prayed them before us, for prayer is not bound by time and space. And this form of prayer is not as elevated as lay people may have been led to believe. It may be true, as some have said, that one can never pray the psalms as they should be prayed without a vision of all the past history of the church and an understanding of its

32

future promise. But there is nothing to stop us from being less ambitious in the meantime and reading the psalms for enjoyment, comfort, and to expand our concept of God. There are among them love poems of exquisite beauty which can say for us, all we may not be able or ready to say for ourselves. Of course, that means being selective and presupposes some kind of knowledge of the Book of Psalms. One way to accomplish that is to read a psalm a day and think about it—meditate on it—then make a choice of those that speak to our experience.

Most of us know at least part of Psalm 23, the song of the Good Shepherd. "The Lord is my shepherd, there is nothing I shall want. . . .," and perhaps Psalm 42, "As the doe longs for running streams, so longs my soul for you, my God." Then there is Psalm 139 with its beautiful imagery: "O Lord, you have probed me and you know me, you know when I stand and when I sit. . . .where could I go to escape your spirit? Where could I flee from your presence? If I climb to heaven you are there. . . .if I flew to the point of sunrise or westward across the sea, your hand would still be guiding me, your right hand holding me. . . ." These are some of the many which elucidate for us God's relationship with his people. But there is a wealth to choose from—150 to be exact—and one to fit every mood, emotion, or experience. We may want to skip some of the stanzas calling down wrath and terrible destruction on enemies or, on second thought, perhaps consider if they do not express, in shocking and graphic terms, sentiments we may secretly have entertained at times towards our own opponents.

A prayer form which calls for inner visualizing is an adaptation of the Ignatian exercises wherein one selects an episode from the gospels and places oneself at the scene, a participant in the action. This may not seem like real prayer, but that is probably only because we are not talking but just allowing Scripture to speak through our senses and imagination. An example of this might be the incident in Matthew's Gospel where Jesus walks on the Sea of Galilee.

The disciples are alone in the boat. Jesus has gone into the hills to pray. Rather than observe the scene as an onlooker, we enter the boat with the disciples, observe their weariness (they have only recently returned from their first evangelistic tour and have had little time to rest) and try to feel it in ourselves.

It is dusk and darkness is falling fast. The night feels warm and at first the breeze is refreshingly brisk. Feel it on our arms and face; feel the heave and sway of the boat beneath us as the sails fill and tug. We are settling down, squatting perhaps on the rough boards in the well of the boat, grateful for the respite, silent or talking quietly, when the wind rises. It is one of those sudden squalls Galilee is notorious for. That's the end of rest for this trip!

By the early hours of morning we're only halfway across the lake. The wind is howling, whipping the sails, stinging the skin with spray, spurting water into burning, bloodshot eyes! The waves are enormous, breaking over the side of the boat. There's an air of grim urgency about the men struggling with the sails and rudder. We feel it too, frantically bailing with whatever comes to hand. We might not make it to daybreak. We're exhausted, soaked to the skin, nervous, anxious.

Suddenly someone cries, "What's that?" What? There, on the water, something white, eerie, glowing, moving towards us. "It's a ghost!" Feel the skin prickle on our bodies; hair stiffen on the nape of the neck. We're in no condition for rational thought. But, above the wind, that beloved voice: "Courage! It's only me." Jesus? Thank God! But how can we be sure?

Peter, foolish, impetuous as always, shouts, "If it really is you, call me to come to you." And Jesus calls "Come." It's amazing! Peter is actually getting out of the boat. His eyes are fixed on Jesus. He's walking on the surface. It's impossible. But he's walking. But there, the wind hits him and he falters. He looks away, down at the waves and— he's going down! "Save me, save me!" we hear him cry, and before we can move Jesus leans down and catches his arms.

Suddenly they are back in the boat. How did it happen? We crowd around—the wind has dropped and the lake is calm as a mill pond. Jesus is looking at Peter. "Why did you doubt?" he says, sadly it seems. "Have you so little faith?" Peter doesn't know what has happened, he just stands looking at Jesus.

Now Jesus looks at us. He doesn't say "Would you have done better?" He doesn't need to. But we have to ask it of ourselves. If we had been the one to whom he said "Come," would we have leapt out in defiance of the laws of physics and walked into the storm? Or stayed rooted to the spot, afraid and rationalizing our fear? Something inside us cringes. Shivering, and not from cold, we know that we have been called. How have we responded to that call?

Basically the idea is to place ourselves within the gospel event and then apply its message to ourselves. We give our imagination free rein to sense the weather conditions and suffer from them; to feel the tiredness, concern, the fear and trembling; to know the shame of inadequacy and faithlessness before Christ.

Once we accept this as a valid form of prayer and one which can greatly increase our understanding of Scripture and its application to us, we are on the way to a greater appreciation of the gospels. Whatever passage we chose, it will never again be possible to hear or read it without a more intimate awareness of both the event and its meaning. Instead of reports of happenings almost 2000 years old, the gospel stories can be transformed into lived experiences of things of eternal significance. And that is what prayer is about.

Meditating on the Our Father is another recommended way of creative praying. After all, the Our Father is Christ's own prayer and we can hardly do better than that. We can take each phrase, reflect on it, explore as far as possible what it means, what images it awakens, repeat it prayerfully and let it seep into our hearts, savoring what it says of God and to us. Perhaps we may prefer to look at it from a new vantage point, pondering why the Apostles asked to be taught to pray and what Jesus meant them to understand. What follows is a personal reflection on the whys and wherefores. It is not meant as a theological comment, but merely as an individual exploration into the prayer.

When the Apostles asked Jesus to teach them to pray, they could not have meant to suggest that they were strangers to prayer. As practicing Jews they must have been familiar with

35

traditional modes of prayer such as the psalms, prayers of thanksgiving, prayers of petititon, and so on. What they were asking must have been something different.

Jesus was an enigma to them most of the time. They shared his life, loved him, and longed to understand him better and be more like him. But even though their backgrounds were similar, he was in many ways a stranger to them. His approach to life was different from theirs; his values were different; his attitude towards people was different; most of all, his relationship with God was well beyond their experience.

Watching him as they did, being with him 24 hours a day, they could hardly have failed to notice the many occasions when he took time out to pray. The more demanding his ministry, the more pressing the crowds, the more he felt—or seemed to feel—the need to withdraw alone to pray. Obviously it occurred to the Apostles that there was a connection between the kind of man Jesus was and his habit of frequent prayer. They must have concluded that his was a different kind of prayer, more evocative, more effective than their own, and more personally fulfilling. Perhaps what they really meant to say was, "If it is your prayer that makes you the kind of person you are, teach us to pray as you pray."

Jesus, answering the yearning of their hearts rather than the spoken word, shared the essence of his prayer by giving them the Our Father and thus led them to an insight into the relationship between God and his people. In effect, he might have said to them:

When you pray, enter into the presence of the Most Holy one who is your loving Father; whose whole desire is that the peace and love living within him should come alive in you too and in all people on earth.

Remember that it is he who gives you life and sustains life in you; whose forgiveness is unfailing, and who calls for reciprocal forgiveness in you. Know that in union with him neither temptation nor the evil of this world will overcome you.

The Apostles had asked for a method of prayer, and Jesus responded to the longing they had not yet learned to verbalize and led them to relationship with God. He did not say, "Prayer is relationship," as one would today. he defined what that means: a heightened consciousness of God as ac-

36

tive, loving, and totally involved in the daily affairs of every human being. And he expressed it in terms of human dependency and the need to live in intimate trustful contact with God.

What was new was not the idea of relationship, but the *kind* of relationship. Prayer, as Jesus taught it in the Our Father and in his own person, was the need of a person, who knew himself intimately loved, to take time to be with the one who loved him and to respond to that love in every aspect of his life. For him there was no great leap from God the Father to God as Lover; they were one. It was the need of one who knew he must be true to his essential being and must align his will always with that of the Father. It was the maturing of relationship, the union of love that overcomes fear and brings peace and integration of mind and soul.

The Our Father is Christ's own word on the Father, the word of the only one who knows him.

Many people today are moving away from traditional prayers of the church simply because they are traditional. This is probably true of prayers of intercession to Mary and the saints. In the last decade or so we have come more to the idea of direct access to God through Christ, and there is not the same devotion to the saints or to Mary as there used to be. But in intercessory prayer we do not pray *to* the saints but *with* them. We should not limit prayer. If our spiritual space is populated with heroes of the faith who became transparent enough for the light of Christ to shine powerfully through them, and if our prayer is united with their still-living prayer, can we fail to be richer for it? After all, the liturgical prayer of the church joins itself with the prayer of the angels and saints in the celebration of the Eucharist, and teaches the spiritual communion of all souls. So those of us who love a particular saint should not hesitate to enlist his or her aid, if it helps us pray. We beginners need all the assistance we can get.

We are, on the whole, a single-visioned lot. We pray as though wearing blinkers, as though one form of prayer precluded others. People will often say emphatically, "Oh, I *always* pray to the Father," or "to Christ," or "to the Holy Spirit," and so on. Why? If we are praying every day and most of the day, we can afford to broaden our base of prayer from time to time. Even if we are very sophisticated and intellectual beginners, we can learn from the church's saints and from the Mother of God. We may even try Trinitarian prayer! Thus even when we pray alone, we can still pray in comunity and come to a clearer understanding of what is meant by the communion of saints.

Those who pray Mary's own prayer, the rosary, often see it as an invisible chain uniting them with people all over the world who also pray it. It is probably the most widespread prayer, after the Our Father, even today. Attempts have been made to compare the rosary with the mantra of eastern religions, but the only resemblance is the superficial one of repetition. The rosary can be prayed with a number of variations, excluding the rapid-fire let's-get-through-with-it approach that has done it so much harm. It can be prayed slowly, reflectively, taking the Our Father and the Hail Mary phrase by phrase. Each repetition of the Hail Mary would concentrate on a different phrase, a different aspect of Mary's place in the life of her son and in the life of the church, and relate it to our own life and problems. This expands the usual 15-minute recitation to about 45 minutes or more. Then there are various ways of meditating on the mysteries, using scriptural readings or visualizing each event. Or one may relate the mysteries to the work of the day, as one commuter does. An example of his use of the rosary is to take each set of mysteries and draw from them guidance for the day, for example:

The Joyful Mysteries
- The Annunciation: May all my pronouncements of this day give joy and comfort to the hearers. May I be careful in my statements and aware of the needs of others.
- The Visitation: May my visits with people during this day be pleasant, bringing accord, friendship, and affection. May they make a difference for good for those I visit.
- The Nativity: May all the ideas generated by me today be useful and positive, full of hope and goodness.
- The Presentation: May those to whom I present myself today find me acceptable and nonthreatening and so be

receptive. if I have to make a presentation of some kind, let me make it as well as I can.
- The Finding in the Temple: Help me find time, Lord, to seek you in my work and leisure this day.

The Sorrowful Mysteries
- The Agony in the Garden: If today has its moments of sadness and testing, Lord, give me your strength.
- The Scourging at the Pillar: No doubt today will bring its barbs, its hurts and pain. Nothing like your sufferings, but help me in my weakness to bear them, Lord.
- The Crowning with Thorns: Even a minor headache hinders me. I am not good at accepting pain. Help me to accept it with you.
- The Carrying of the Cross: Lord, you told us that each day we must deny ourselves and carry our cross. Help me when I falter, when I fail you today.
- The Crucifixion and Death of Jesus: I must be prepared to suffer the death of my own desires again today, Lord. It is nothing like your death, yet there is something of your death in it. Let me deny myself with you, die with you, and in you, rise again.

The Glorious Mysteries
- The Resurrection: Lord, awaken my spirit, my dedication. Let your will be done, not mine.
- The Ascension: Carry my spirit with you, Lord, so that as the day progresses and I am feeling low, you will raise me up.
- The Descent of the Holy Spirit: Let your Spirit rest on me in a special way today, so that the decisions I make will be the right ones, helpful to others and to you.
- The Assumption: Lord, help me transcend myself so that I may be equal to what you want of me this day.
- The Coronation of Mary: This day, let me follow the example of your Mother and the saints, so that I may be truly Christian.

This form lends itself to a very personal application and can be used simply as a meditation on the mysteries or in conjunction with the recitation of the whole rosary. This commuter had an hour to fill between home and work, but those with shorter journeys can experiment with their own variations.

It may come as a surprise to some that prayer to the Holy Spirit was not inaugurated with the charismatic renewal, but a glance at the prayers of the Mass and the writings of Church Fathers will reassure us that the Holy Spirit has been vital to the church ever since Pentecost. Today more people than ever are praying for the blessing of the Spirit in what is known as charismatic prayer. Although this has become associated with praying in tongues, glossolalia is not always part of charismatic prayer. The gifts of the Spirit are many and varied, and their outward manifestations are not as important as inner strengthening and conversion.

The purpose of charismatic prayer is to release the power of the Holy Spirit within a person, so that the Spirit, in effect, prays with him or her. Speaking in tongues is believed to be the articulation of this prayer. It is not necessary to understand what one is saying—indeed, it may not be a recognizable language—for the understood object is praise and thanksgiving. The greatest significance of this form of prayer is that it leads a person to a deeper desire for prayer and to a hunger for the Scriptures. This, of course, is the aim of all prayer and, when it is accompanied by a humble acceptance of God's inscrutable will, it inevitably conforms a person more closely to God's vision.

Listening to music is an another excellent aid to prayer as long as the music is not too raucous and nerve-jangling. Many symphonies, nocturnes, and other classical forms of music can produce deeply meditative moods, from which it is easy to slip into prayer. Praying through instrumental concerts and programs of song brings the love of music to where it belongs, and can raise us to that height of emotional and spiritual experience we call a peak.

We are used to sung prayer in hymns and renditions of the psalms; but, really, any reasonably good love song can be sung as a prayer when God is our focus. Many of the oldies like "Ah Sweet Mystery of Life," "Love's Old Sweet Song," "Love Is My Reason for Living," "At Dawning," and so on, could almost have been written first as prayers. Then there are modern hits such as "I Don't Know How to Love Him," from *Jesus Christ Superstar,* the Oscar-winning

"Ready to Take a Chance Again," "If I Loved You," and many more. The songs assail us in every store, restaurant, cinema, and from every radio station. Even busy teenagers might listen to them from a new angle to see how many could apply to their relationship with God. Those that are blatantly inappropriate obviously have nothing to do with love, however much they may pretend to have. The little habit of using popular music for prayers would not only put the endless airing of songs to good use, but would also help us analyze the kind of material we are listening to day in and day out. Many of the extravagant claims of love songs make sense only when applied to the love of God, and we can learn a great deal about the kinds of needs and longings that tug at us by listening to the songs in this light. Music moves us; we might as well be moved in the right direction.

Prayer is out of place nowhere. if a situation does not seem suitable for prayer, the answer is not to avoid prayer but to change the situation. After all, we do not blind God to what we are doing by not thinking about him. The whole problem with finding time to pray, or not finding it, is that we are so closed-minded about it, and try to confine prayer to the corners of our lives. Sometimes the idea of prayer is so separated from normal living that we assume special attitudes and facial expressions for it. When someone says, "Let us pray," it is often as though a hand had wiped all expression from our faces except heavy solemnity or a sighing sanctity—unless we happen to be in church, and then we merely continue to look bored. In contrast, when a friend says, "Let's talk a while," we usually look up eagerly, accepting with pleasure. We do not always have to be so serious in prayer. It is permissible to laugh with God and take real pleasure in his company. Where did we get our sense of humor and fun from, if not from him?

We are usually quite unaware of the prejudices with which we approach the act of praying. A friend who was at one time an Episcopalian minister but has since converted to Catholicism, once startled us by inviting us to pray then and there when one of us complained about a physical ailment. "You mean here—now?" our unfortunate sufferer asked uneasily. *Here* was on a sidewalk. *Now* was as we were leaving for home after a retreat. Our friend said with amused understanding, "Well, we could go back into the room we just left." And so we did, and hands were laid on and prayers were said and the whole thing was most un-Catholic!

Since then, of course, healing services and prayers have become prevalent in the church, and we have become used to that kind of thing, but at that time it was something of a shock. Such spontaneous praying does not come to us readily even today, and yet it is wholly Christian in character. Most of us really do need to become less self-conscious and more God-conscious in prayer.

This is probably a major rule to be observed in any prayer community, even if it involves only two or three people. There is a tendency to fall into didactic terms when praying aloud, as if the object were to teach others. But we are not praying to impress or edify our companions; we are there to join with them in conversation with God. Since before God we know so little, how can we teach? Before God each person's prayer is equally worthwhile and equally to be respected. He meets each of us on a different plane but he always meets us. So no individual should hog the available time or panic at the sound of silence, but let pauses last long enough to encourage the shy ones to a verbal breakthrough.

Today, more than ever, people want to pray and to pray together. Perhaps we always did; perhaps it was just that too many of us were afraid to suggest it. But times change and customs change, and we are so socially minded nowadays that it is time for prayer to make its debut on our social scene.

Whether we pray alone or communally, vocally or silently, verbally or in mute spiritual longing for God, unimaginatively or with inner visualizing, in snacks or four-course-meals, traditionally or spontaneously, in our own words or in grateful acceptance of someone else's, there is a tremendous variety of prayer forms to choose from. So many, perhaps, as to be intimidating. But boldness in prayer is a great virtue and we must remember that God cherishes our prayer primarily in our will to pray and in our longing for union with him. So, like Peter, we can afford to be foolish and naive and plunge unafraid into the waters of our own prayer without being too disturbed about the waiting depths. We'll start to sink only as we begin to worry about how we're doing rather than keeping our eyes on God, Father and Son.

What is there
to pray about?

"If we don't change God's mind, what is the point of praying?" What indeed? Prayer certainly changes things, and if we haven't been twisting God's arm, what have we been doing? Let us hope we have felt a twinge or two in our own muscles and a few pains of metamorphosis. Many of us would become indignant at the accusation that we think we know better than God, yet we pray exactly as if we did. "Don't let this happen; do this; do that. It would be much better if such and such were to come about. Don't do this; don't do that!" Our anger and frustration when prayers are not answered as we expect emphasize that we really do think we know best.

Sooner or later we have to grow to spiritual adulthood, or at least to advanced adolescence, and move from the "gimme" to the "take-me" concept. Prayer is for ourselves, but not in the narrow sense of personal gratification and consolation only. It is for ourselves in the context of social responsibility and universal human need. We are involved with the entire human race and our prayer should witness to that.

John Donne's perception of the bond between all human beings is essentially Christian. "I am involved in mankind" not only in such physical or material objectives as caring for the sick and aged, feeding the hungry and the poor, clothing the ragged, or healing the abused. I am involved in mankind through a spiritual interrelatedness that implies an intensely personal obligation to pray and love so that the power of accepting, transforming compassion is activated and liberated through me to radiate, touch other lives, and so change the world little by little, piece by piece.

Every little act of Christian kindness, every warm accepting move towards others, every active prayer that we perform in our own small circle of concern must affect others, spreading like ripples from a pebble thrown into a pool. A young hitchhiker said it very well after being welcomed and cared for in a little mountain community and warmly accepted by its pastor: "How can I thank you for all your kindness except by taking it with me and spreading it wherever I go?"

We are indentured in a universal mission to enlighten and sanctify our own lives and, as far as is in our power, those of our fellow human beings. As long as we perceive prayer or love as a purely individual affair, our prayer will not be Christian prayer nor our love Christian love. Prayer does not begin nor end with us. The failure to comprehend this is probably why, more than 19 centuries after Christ, the world is still not Christian. The billion or so people who claim to be Christ's followers, far from healing the wounds of hatred, violence, and indignity, have in far too many cases exacerbated them. The sad truth, it seems, is that the vast majority of Christians simply have not understood the Christian vocation. Our whole religious consciousness has centered on the goal of personal salvation rather than on the realization of the Kingdom of God on earth. Not too long ago an adult education class was asked what particular benefit there was in being a Catholic as opposed to being a member of some other Christian denomination. Why, they were asked, do you remain in the church? Almost 75 percent answered that being Catholic gave them an edge on heaven. Many people feel like that about prayer as well.

Personal salvation is not what prayer and the Christian vocation are really about. They are about mirroring God in ourselves, in the community of the church, in the world, and in the way we live in the world. St. Gregory of Nyssa wrote long ago that to pray is to convert one's whole life. It was, he said, the only thing worth doing with the whole of our being and the whole of our time. Mirroring God, as he phrased it, is what we exist for and that means also seeing from God's viewpoint, caring about what is going on in the world and feeling compassion for all who share it with us.

Even reading newspapers and listening to radio or television can, strange as it may seem, have a vital place in spiritual development. The daily dose of crime, catastrophe, violence, and abuse of human dignity that parades through the ether calls for more than to be ignored or clucked over and forgotten. The scene of an accident might spur a prayer for the well-being of those involved. The terrible toll of such

44

things as hurricanes, brush fires, or floods could move us to prayers of both thanksgiving for our own exemption and concern for the victims. This is the human predicament in which we are involved and it is part of us, too.

From God's viewpoint there are a lot of suffering people out there and his love does not discriminate. We are called to care about and pray for criminals as well as victims, abusers as well as abused, privileged as well as underprivileged. In a checkout line at a supermarket a woman was heard expressing pity for a highly-publicized and wealthy socialite whose life has been extraordinarily tragic. Her companion snorted, "Her? No, I'm not sorry for her. She has 20 million dollars!" But even the fabulously rich are people to be loved, forgiven their wealth, and included in our prayer. And often that requires a complete turnaround in our habit of thinking.

Some genuinely good people are shocked by the suggestion that Christian compassion is no respecter of persons and requires that we love and forgive the Charles Mansons as well as their victims, the Idi Amins as well as those who suffer their rule, the perverted and the spiritually handicapped. Our prayer is meant to reach out to such unhappy human beings, and our inability to sincerely embrace their need as our own is yet another matter to pray about.

> Lord, fill me with your generosity and forgiveness so that they may overcome the fear that makes me recoil from these companions on the pilgrimage through life who, in their deformity of spirit, destroy life and assault the dignity of your people. Help me to love them as you have loved me and continue to love me despite my own faults and aberrations.

Once prayer and love have been offered there is no way to take them back, and they move beyond our control to add weight to the balance of good and evil. The world needs our love and prayer to counteract the hatred, despair, and callousness that so afflict our race. Without such awareness we can grow disheartened and despondent, feeling that we are not getting anything out of prayer. But prayer is never static. There are fluctuations, highs and lows, and they are related to our spiritual and emotional condition at the time.

Holding on to the broad perspective of prayer helps us

weather the dry, difficult times. Some people after deep and persistent prayer will experience a whole new dimension of love and prayer that goes beyond their grasp and gains a momentum of its own to the degree that it is united with God's love. We should be prepared to let this happen and allow prayer and love to flow unhindered without trying to manipulate or limit the effect. "Love is only love when you give it away," and we must be prepared to let love and prayer go once we have launched them and trust God to do what he will with them.

In those periods when we don't feel like praying or think there is nothing to pray about, chances are that a quiet thought about family or friends will turn up a few areas of concern or gratitude that can be readily prayed over. Then again, the future of local or national government is never so secure that prayers for our leaders are likely to be redundant. Probably those very times when we feel least like praying are the times which are potentially broadening and can direct our prayer where it has not gone before.

In the secularism of this modern age, when beliefs are so often challenged and religion ridiculed, Christians need to keep this kind of vision before them. However hectic our days, we need to pause periodically, recall God's presence, and think again of the reason why we live and what our lives are meant to accomplish. This kind of orientation of spirit, this continuous, living prayer, is the one way to reach and maintain equilibrium in the uncertainties of this century and to bring events into their proper relationship. The pressures under which most of us labor today often distort our values, so that many things appear important which, in the long run, do not really matter. And, conversely, many things that are of lasting and transcendent value now seem irrelevant. But when prayer, that is, the heightened consciousness of God's nearness, forms the focal point of all we do and strive to be, it becomes the corrective lens that enables us to see things as they are, rectifies moral and spiritual astigmatism, and relieves the stress it brings about. Christian prayer is never only something we say but something we live and are.

No one today demonstrates this as well as Mother Teresa of Calcutta, that little woman who stands so firmly in contradiction to the things of the world but through whom the love of Christ reaches out to everyone she meets, rich and poor alike. She is often referred to as a living saint. She would probably scorn the title. She is what she professes to be, a Christian. Christ's words come alive in her and dominate her life. Her prayer and love are wholly integrated into her being. In her, prayer life and actual life are the same thing; there is neither division nor distinction. She seems to bask in God's presence almost unceasingly, and yet she is a tirelessly busy woman and plagued with ill health. People are changed by her. Pagans, Christians, Muslims, people of all persuasions are moved to re-evaluate their lives and beliefs after encountering her.

Mother Teresa's ministry to the dying is not one that could be called personally rewarding. The people she ministers to are seldom physically healed; mostly they die. Her healing is a different kind. It is Christ's kind of healing, the healing of the human spirit. The terrible scenes of human deprivation and neglect in which she works do not seem to rouse her to bitterness, only to sorrow. The psychiatrist Abraham Maslow would no doubt have classified her as a self-actualized person: what we would call a mature human being; what by Christ's definition is a Christian. her witness assures us that it is possible to come to human maturity. It is possible to be Christian in the fullest sense. But it requires that we spend time in the presence of God and are willing to let his love do its work in us.

Tying it all together

Carefree contemplatives or bustling busy folk, we all are required to face the challenge of tying together the loose ends and broken threads of our lives and weaving them into the whole cloth of complete humanness, which means emotional and spiritual maturity. We may not all complete the task, but the object is to do as well as possible in our particular circumstances. And we should be prepared for loneliness. No matter how many advisors, counselors or directors may stand over us, ultimately we alone are the weavers. Prayer is the loom and we sit at it alone in the presence of God. We may begin mechanically and with uncertainty, but as we grow more adept and confident we may find deeper meaning and inspiration. Then, as a discernible pattern emerges, it becomes possible to visualize the whole cloth of our living and mission as God has always seen it.

St. John, in his gospel account of the crucifixion, speaks of Jesus being clothed in a garment of one piece, woven from neck to hem without seam, a flawless cloth of sufficient value for the soldiers to squabble over who should have it. It seems symbolic that Jesus, the one wholly mature human being, in whom body, mind, and spirit were fully integrated, should have been dressed in a whole cloth, a perfect and skillful piece of weaving, each thread woven continuously, neither cut nor sewn nor marred in any way. And it seems significant that John thought it important enough to mention.

So it is appropriate to suggest that whatever we do with our lives and whatever they do to us, however torn apart and fragmented our personalities may become, prayer is the one way to tie the ends together and weave what we are into the whole cloth of Christ-centered humanness. That means searching out an acute and growing acceptance of God as friend and lover. It means understanding the human vocation as bringing to realization God's image in ourselves. Without this awareness anyone can justify not praying because of lack of time, at least to his or her own satisfaction. But with such awareness, prayer becomes a major priority and the orientation of life.